*Horrid History of Beauty*

# DANGEROUS DIETS

## ANITA CROY

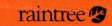
raintree

a Capstone company — publishers for children

Raintree is an imprint of Capstone Global Library Limited, a company incorporated in England and Wales having its registered office at 264 Banbury Road, Oxford, OX2 7DY – Registered company number: 6695582

**www.raintree.co.uk**
myorders@raintree.co.uk

Produced for Raintree by Calcium
Editors: Sarah Eason and Tim Cooke
Designers: Clare Webber and Lynne Lennon
Picture researcher: Rachel Blount
Originated by Capstone Global Library Ltd
Printed and bound in India

ISBN 978 1 4747 7764 3 (hardback)
ISBN 978 1 4747 7767 4 (paperback)

**British Library Cataloguing in Publication Data**
A full catalogue record for this book is available from the British Library.

**Acknowledgements**
We would like to thank the following for permission to reproduce photographs: Cover: Shutterstock: Anastasia Sitnikova; Inside: Flickr: Joe Wolf: p. 32; Library of Congress: George Grantham Bain Collection: p. 34; Paul Fornier: p. 24; Shutterstock: Africa Studio: p. 5t; AlessandroBiascioli: p. 39; Best_photo_studio: p. 11b; Francesco Dazzi: p. 42; Tatyana Dzemileva: p. 41t; Everett Historical: p. 30; FashionStock.com: p. 40; Joe Gough: p. 28; Peter Lorimer: p. 10; Meagan Marchant: p. 8; Ekaterina Markelova: p. 43t; MidoSemsem: p. 6; Moxumbic: p. 19b; Neelsky: p. 9; Photo and Vector: p. 43b; Ekaterina Pokrovsky: p. 12; Redhen: p. 5b; RS Picture: p.19t; Aizuddin Saad: p. 15; Sorbis: pp. 1, 38; Swapan Photography: p 37t; Matthew J Thomas: p. 17; Debby Wong: p. 41b; Wikimedia Commons: p. 26; Pieter Aertsen: p. 18; Ollie Atkins: p. 37b; Jacopo de' Barbari: p. 16b; William Clark: p. 23; Line engraving by F. Clerici/ Wellcome Images: p. 16c; Elliott & Fry: p. 27b; Enric: p. 4; Evan-Amos: p. 25t; Theodore H. Feder: p. 11t; John Gilroy: p. 31b; Jules-Alexandre Grün: p. 29; after Hans Holbein: p. 20; Charles Hulpeau: p. 21; Rob Koopman: p. 7b; Thomas Lawrence: p. 25b; Per Meistrup: p. 14; Mogana Das Murtey and Patchamuthu Ramasamy: p. 36; Marie-Lan Nguyen: p. 7t; Pamperchu: p. 33t; Jean Paris early 1900s: p. 27t; workshop of Peter Paul Rubens: p. 22; Walter Dendy Sadler: p. 13; U.S. National Archives and Records Administration: p. 31t; United States Office of War Information, Overseas Picture Division: p. 35; Wellcome Images: p. 33b.

# -CONTENTS-

# Chapter 1

# ANCIENT
## - DIETS -

*The earliest humans found food in the wild.*
*They hunted animals and gathered nuts and berries.*
*It was only when people learned how*
*to grow crops that there was food to spare.*

This did not happen quickly. It took our ancestors around 2.6 million years to move from hunting and gathering to growing crops such as wheat, barley, corn and rice.

## START OF FARMING

Hunter-gatherers ate a diet made up of about one-third meat and fish and two-thirds plants, nuts and seeds. (A popular modern diet is based on similar proportions of food. It is called the Paleo diet, short for "Palaeolithic", meaning "from the early Stone Age".) The population moved around to find animals and plants. Hunting was difficult, however, so hunters often came home without food. Plants and berries were more reliable sources of food. The combination of lots of plants and an occasional bit of meat suited humans.

Early peoples painted hunting scenes in caves. The paintings may have been an appeal for help from the gods in the hunt.

The coming of agriculture changed people's diet and had important effects on society. With more food available, more children survived to adulthood, so the population grew. People also started to live in settled communities near their fields. Population growth led to the emergence of cities and then to early **civilizations**. But when humans moved to eating a diet based mainly on grain crops, they lost some **nutritional** variety. They suffered from a lack of iron. When farmers started keeping cattle, they introduced **parasites** and **infectious** diseases.

Women and children often gathered berries and nuts while men went hunting.

## OVEREATING

As soon as humans had enough to eat, some people started to eat too much. The fear of not knowing where the next meal was coming from was part of the human personality. After millions of years of being slim, people started to grow fat. Soon, people in early societies began to worry that they were eating too much. It was the ancient Greeks and Romans who first made a direct link between what people ate and maintaining good general health and fitness.

The introduction of farmed crops was a turning point in human history.

# ROOTS OF
## - HEALTHY EATING -

*It seems that ancient peoples knew a thing or two about being healthy. The ancient Greek diet and love of exercise was the perfect combination for a long life.*

The ancient Greeks knew a lot about food. The word "diet" comes from the Greek word *diaita*, which means "a way of life". The Greek diaita was living well by exercising and eating the right things. The Greeks had it all worked out 3,000 years ago.

## A GREEK DINER

In the fourth century BC, the physician Hippocrates made the connection between "**calories** in and calories out"– in other words, taking energy in as food and burning it off through exercise. Hippocrates realized that people were healthiest when they ate moderately and moved around. He wrote, "Man cannot live healthily on food without a certain amount of exercise." The more you ate, the more you had to exercise.

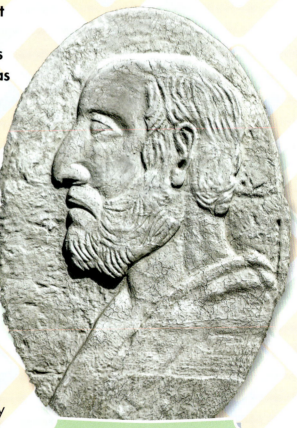

Hippocrates is called the founder of medicine. Doctors today still take the Hippocratic Oath to promise to care for their patients.

## NO BEANS FOR YOU!

The sixth-century BC philosopher and mathematician Pythagoras attracted many followers who formed a sort of cult. Pythagoras instructed his followers not to eat meat. That means they were the first people we know of to become **vegetarians** by choice. Pythagoras also forbade his followers from eating any type of bean. One theory for this is that he believed that beans caused gas (true!) and that when a person broke wind a piece of their soul escaped (false!).

For the Greeks, having an athletic body was highly desirable.

# hello beautiful

Wealthy ancient Egyptians were on a fast track to an early grave. Their diet was full of artery-clogging **saturated fats**. Queen Hatshepsut, for example, was **obese** and suffered from **diabetes**. Also, the bodies of Egyptian priests have clogged arteries and damaged hearts from too much beef, cake and alcohol. That's because the priests ate the rich food that was offered to the gods every day!

Hatshepsut was only the second woman to become ruler of Egypt.

# DON'T EAT
## - THAT! -

One of the earliest guides to what to eat came from religious texts. Different religions banned different foods. Things could get quite confusing!

The religious texts of Judaism and Islam – the Torah and the Quran – set out strict dietary rules for their followers. Pork was – and still is – strictly off the menu. It was believed that pork was "impure" because pigs ate rubbish and waste in ancient settlements.

## PIGS VS CHICKENS

Historically there might be practical reasons why both religions banned eating pork. Both Judaism and Islam began in the hot, dry Middle East. Pigs need a lot of water to survive, and it is not always available there. When they are killed, they produce a lot of meat. In the heat, however, the meat would go bad before people had time to eat it all. Compared with pigs, chickens need much less water to survive. Chickens also lay eggs and are smaller, so a whole chicken can be eaten before the meat goes off. Both Judaism and Islam allow their followers to eat chicken and eggs.

In hot countries, chickens are easier to keep than pigs as they need less water.

## SACRED COWS

There are more dietary restrictions in India. Hindus believe that cows are sacred because the goddess Kamdhenu took the form of a cow on Earth. As a result, no **devout** Hindus eat beef. Cows are also allowed to wander freely. Even on busy streets in Indian cities, cows walk alongside buses, cars and rickshaws!

Other religions ban meat-eating completely. Buddhists and Indians who follow a faith called Jainism only eat food that has not been harmed. Jains will not eat anything that has been grown below ground, such as onions or carrots. They believe the plant is harmed when it is pulled out of the ground.

Hindus in India decorate cows for holy festivals as a sign that the animals are sacred.

## to die for

Cannibalism (eating the meat of other humans) is condemned by most religions. Until the nineteenth century, however, some Pacific peoples ate humans in religious ceremonies. People have sometimes eaten other people to avoid starvation. In 1972, for example, members of a Uruguayan rugby team ate their dead companions while they waited for rescue after an air crash in the Andes mountains. Cannibalism is not illegal, but it is illegal to kill a person in order to eat them.

# HAVE ANOTHER
## - DORMOUSE -

*The Romans liked to splash their cash on food and drink. Holding lavish dinners and parties was a sign of being wealthy.*

Stories of the Romans' excessive eating and drinking have been endlessly retold through history – but the stories were not always fair.

### LET'S THROW UP!

Most of these stories focused on how greedy the Romans were. In the first century AD, the author Petronius described a feast hosted by a former slave who had become rich. To show off his wealth, he served dormice cooked in honey and poppy seeds, boar and **suckling pigs**, and a flying rabbit! According to one story, the Romans built special rooms called vomitoriums. They supposedly went there to throw up when they were full to bursting – so they could eat more. But these rooms did not really exist. In fact, *vomitorium* is Latin for an exit from an **amphitheatre**. It is based on a word meaning "spewing out". Perhaps that is where the false connection came from.

The Roman diet was based on flat, round loaves of bread, eaten with cheese and wine.

## I'M STUFFED!

Most ordinary Romans ate three meals a day. Their staple food was a flat type of bread made from a grain called emmer. They dipped the bread in wine and ate it with cheese and olives. They could not afford meat, fish, fruit, eggs and milk.

Some Romans did eat far too much. One senator was so fat that he could only walk if two of his slaves carried his belly! King Dionysius of Heraclea ate so much that he was always sleepy. He had to be pricked with needles to keep him awake.

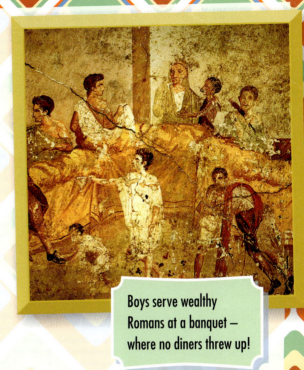

Boys serve wealthy Romans at a banquet — where no diners threw up!

# hello beautiful

Marcus Gavius Apicius lived in the first century AD. He loved food so much that he once sailed from Rome to Libya just to eat some shrimp. Apicius gave his name to one of the first cookbooks in history. Famous for his lavish banquets, he was eventually bankrupted by his luxurious lifestyle. He took poison rather than eat ordinary food.

Marcus Gavius Apicius was disappointed with the famed shrimp of Libya.

# Chapter 2
# THE MIDDLE
## - AGES -

*The Middle Ages in Europe were
all about farming. Most families worked on
the land growing crops for their master and
a few for themselves.*

**The diet of a medieval peasant – which was nearly everyone – was dull.
Peasants lived on turnips, and a lot of bread and beer. Wealthier people
got to eat suckling pig and fish, and to drink wine as well as beer.**

## WHAT'S FOR DINNER?

It was desirable to look plump, because it was a sign of wealth. The poor
were always thin, because they did not eat enough. An eleventh-century
Persian physician called Avicenna had tips for the overweight. He said
they should fill up with bulky food with little nutritional value, then swallow
**laxatives** and exercise like mad to lose weight.

Vegetable gardens could be
decorative, like this re-created
medieval garden in France.

Monks enjoy a feast in the late Middle Ages, by which time they had become famous for their luxurious lifestyle.

## SLIM IS GOOD

The idea that being slim is "better" than being fat may have begun with Christianity. Around AD 500, a Roman noble called Benedict dedicated his life to Christianity and founded a monastery. Benedict believed monks had to avoid **gluttony** and control their emotions. Benedictine monks ate plain black bread and vegetables washed down with beer once a day. (Nobody drank water, because it was dirty and caused illness.)

## INNOVATIONS

Around AD 1100, European knights went to fight Muslims in the Middle East. The spices they brought home became a status symbol. The rich used candied fruit, sauces and spices to disguise the taste of meat that had gone off. Medieval recipe books began to appear with dietary tips. The fifteenth-century Italian known as Il Platina wrote the first modern best-seller, *De honesta voluptate et valetudine*. The book contained a combination of tasty ("voluptate") and healthy ("valetudine") recipes.

# THAT FOOD WILL
## - KILL YOU! -

In medieval Japan, some Buddhist monks used food as a way to preserve their bodies. It was a long and horrific process that carried on into the twentieth century.

The process of preserving dead bodies by drying them out was not new. The ancient Egyptians had turned dead bodies into **mummies** in this way for thousands of years. But apart from a few cases in India and China, nobody had thought to preserve themselves while they were still alive.

## MUMMIES ALIVE!

In the twelfth century AD, a group of Buddhist monks in Japan decided they would do just that. The monks were extremely religious. They believed that successfully preserving their bodies while they were still alive was the ultimate proof of their devotion. They must have been committed, because the process was very unpleasant. In addition, it took 3,000 days – more than eight years! However, they believed that by the end of the process they would become **immortal**.

The body of one mummified monk is still kept at a monastery in Japan. It is over 800 years old.

## HOW DID THEY DO IT?

The monks dried out their flesh by using extreme dieting. They stopped eating anything that contained fat and moisture, such as soya, wheat and other cereals. Instead they ate nuts, berries, pine needles, and the bark and **resin** of trees. They ate pebbles from the river and herbs to keep their bodies from becoming infected with disease. They also drank tea made from sticky tree sap that was usually used to make **lacquer**. Over time, their bodies dried out from lack of moisture (the average human is 60 per cent water). After 3,000 days of dieting, the monks were buried alive. They were usually closed into a tomb with an air opening. The tomb was then sealed. After a three-year wait, the tomb was opened up to discover if the monk's body was preserved – or if it had decayed.

## to die for

Many religions have required their devotees to fast (go without food and drink). Native Americans fasted when they undertook a **vision quest**. In the Catholic Church, people traditionally fasted for forty days during Lent, a period before Easter. Islam still requires its followers to fast from sunrise to sunset during Ramadan, and Jewish people fast on special religious days.

Muslims in Indonesia gather at sunset during Ramadan to share their first meal of the day.

# THE FIRST
## - DIETS -

Since Il Platina offered his dietary advice in the fifteenth century, diet books have been big business as ordinary people looked to "experts" for advice.

Today, shelves in bookshops and libraries groan with books about dieting, and they often top the bestseller lists. The idea of writing a guide to losing weight dates back to the sixteenth century.

### READ ALL ABOUT IT!

The first best-selling diet book was *The Art of Living*, written in 1558 by the Venetian merchant Luigi Cornaro. Its message was simple: eat everything in moderation.

Luigi Cornaro began to diet to prolong his life.

Cornaro was from Venice. Venice was a key port in the trade with Asia, so it had many spices for cooking.

VENETIE
MD

## MODERATION IN ALL THINGS!

Cornaro had learned his lesson the hard way. He had eaten and drunk everything he wanted for the first 40 years of his life. As he grew older, however, he saw many of his friends die as a result of their **indulgent** and excessive lifestyles. If he wanted to live a long time, Cornaro decided, there was only one way to achieve it. He put himself on a diet.

Cornaro cut his daily intake of food to no more than 400 grams (12 ounces) of bread, soup, eggs and meat, and just 500 millilitres (14 ounces) of wine. As he lost weight and got older, he decided that even this was too much to consume. As an old man, when he wrote his diet book, he sometimes ate just one egg a day. It worked because he lived to the age of either 98 or 102, according to different sources. His book is still in print today!

## hello beautiful

An Italian **noblewoman** called Catherine de Medici changed European eating habits when she married a French prince in the sixteenth century. When she moved to France, she introduced the French to all sorts of things, including olive oil, eating with a fork, putting flowers on the dinner table and wines from her home region of Chianti in Italy.

Putting displays of flowers on the table while eating became a common practice.

# Chapter 3

# THE EARLY
## - MODERN WORLD -

*During the sixteenth century, many of the foods we take for granted today appeared in the West for the first time. Most people were too poor to afford them.*

The early modern age was a time of exciting food discoveries. New foods from around the world included spices, sugar, potatoes and tomatoes. They were imported from distant lands – and were therefore expensive.

## I'M HUNGRY!

As in the Middle Ages, peasants ate dark bread and drank ale. Only the rich ate luxurious white bread. A special treat for the lower classes was stew made from roots, leaves, seeds, nuts and berries. The ingredients were soaked in water to make the stew easier to digest.

This sixteenth-century painting shows meat on a stall in a market. Most people could only afford to eat meat on special occasions.

Turmeric was a popular spice for its taste and its colour. It was also said to have health benefits.

Meanwhile, the rich enjoyed banquets that included hundreds of different dishes such as swan and peacock flavoured with fresh flowers. In the past, people had sweetened food and drinks with honey. Now honey was replaced by "white gold" – sugar. Sugar was introduced to Europe from the Middle East in the eleventh century during the **Crusades**. Fewer than 40 years after Christopher Columbus sailed to North America in 1492, Europeans began growing sugar in the Caribbean, which became a major source of sugar.

## A GAME CHANGER

In 1536, Spanish **conquistadors** conquered the Incas of Peru. Along with gold and silver, they discovered the potato. The Inca had grown potatoes for centuries. Later in the century, the potato appeared in Europe. The English explorer Sir Walter Raleigh planted potatoes on his land in Ireland in 1589. Within 40 years the potato was popular across Europe. Easy to grow, potatoes were filling and nutritious. They soon became the staple food of the poor. The rich had no need for potatoes. For them, the key ingredients were spices to add flavour to dull dishes. Their cooks prepared food using cinnamon, pepper, mustard, cloves and saffron. Such spices were not just flavourings – they were a status symbol.

The potato was easy to grow in the damp, mild climate of northern Europe.

# OUTSIZED
## - RULERS -

King Henry VIII was as famous for his huge appetite as for his different wives. His expanding waistline demonstrated just what happened when you ate and didn't exercise!

Henry had a large appetite for everything! He wore out eight horses a day when he was hunting. When he was not riding, he was dancing or jousting. He ate and drank huge amounts. That worked well until Henry was hurt in a riding accident at the age of 44.

### A HUGE APPETITE

Henry could no longer exercise – but he kept eating. His weight ballooned and his waist reached 137 centimetres (54 inches)! The reason is clear. It was documented that one meal for Henry included soup, herring, cod, lampreys (eels), pike, salmon, whiting, haddock, plaice, bream, porpoise, seal, carp, trout, crabs, lobsters, custard, tart, fritters and fruit. And that was just the first course!

In 1536 Henry VIII was thrown from his horse and left unconscious for two hours. Afterwards, he could no longer do any sort of exercise.

## IT'S A FEAST

Henry wasn't the only monarch to enjoy large meals. In the seventeenth century, King Charles II was obsessed with his weight. He weighed himself many times a day, noting down his weight gains and losses. He noted that he lost over 900 grams (2 pounds) playing tennis, but soon put it back on. It's hardly surprising! At one of Charles's banquets in 1671, the first course alone contained 145 separate dishes.

For a non-monarch, a lavish banquet could have dire consequences. The French finance minister Nicolas Fouquet was thrown in prison in 1661 after he threw such an extravagant banquet that it was clear he was stealing from his employer, King Louis XIV.

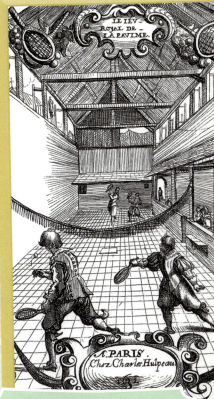

The original form of tennis became popular with Europe's nobles in the sixteenth century.

# hello beautiful

King Adolf Frederick of Sweden ate himself to death – literally! On 12 February 1771, the king sat down to a meal of lobster, caviar, kippers and sauerkraut. He washed down the food with gallons of champagne. Adolf Frederick still had room for dessert. In fact, he ate 14 servings of sweet roll stuffed with almond paste and cream. The king soon felt unwell, not surprisingly. He died shortly after!

[21]

# VOLUPTUOUS
## - BEAUTIES -

The link between beauty and getting enough to eat created a new beauty ideal during the Renaissance and beyond. Plump was the look to go for.

In the first decades of the seventeenth century, a Flemish painter called Peter Paul Rubens painted many women with full, curvy figures. He gave his name to a type of female figure still known today as "Rubenesque".

## RUBENESQUE BEAUTY

Many historians think that Rubens single-handedly made big beautiful, because women took centre stage in his paintings. His inspiration came from the ancient Greek ideals of beauty. He wanted to portray women with natural curves. For Rubens, the fleshy women he painted were a lot more attractive than the people he saw every day. In northern Europe at that time, there were many unhealthy and unattractive people with large pot bellies and stick-like legs.

Rubens painted his wife, Helena Fourment, many times and used her as a model for his paintings.

## BIG IS BEAUTIFUL

At different times in history, or in different cultures around the world, large women have frequently been seen as more beautiful than thin women. In Nigeria, for example, plumpness was so valued by the Efik people that they built special fattening huts. Young girls stayed in the huts until they were plump enough to get married. Some cultures have seen thinness as a sign of sickness and poverty. To be fat was a sign that you had more than enough to eat, which meant you must be rich. Full-figured women were also seen as being more fertile than thin women. Today, on Polynesian islands such as Fiji and Tonga, bigger women and men are both seen as being attractive. On many Caribbean islands, large women are also more fashionable.

## to die for

Until the 1600s, Europeans used honey to sweeten their food. Sugar came to Europe from the Muslim world. People treated it as an exotic spice with healing properties. It was used as medicine. It was so expensive it was only eaten on special occasions. Two centuries later, sugar was imported from America. It was much cheaper, and people were eating twenty times as much sugar as in the past.

Slaves take sugar cane to be processed at a mill in the Caribbean.

# Chapter 4

# THE NINETEENTH
## - CENTURY -

*In the industrial world, the human body was seen as an engine and food was seen as its fuel. Being thin was thought of as being modern, so diets were all the rage.*

Men led the way. In the 1820s they tried all sorts of crazy **fad** diets based on the example of the fashionable English poet, Lord Byron. Thin was in. In the quest to be thin, people tried swallowing diet powders, lard, washing powder and even strychnine – a deadly poison!

## IT'S A MAN'S WORLD

The strange diets included one introduced in about 1900 by the US entrepreneur Horace Fletcher. Fletcher was nicknamed the "Great Masticator" (mastication means chewing), and his diet was known as the "chewing craze". Fletcher advised chewing every piece of food about 100 times before spitting out whatever was left. Dinner parties were not much fun. People spent so much time chewing that there was no chance to chat. At least trips to the toilet were kept to a minimum. With no food being digested, there was little waste to be expelled. Fletcher carried around his smell-free **stools** as proof of how effective his diet was!

Horace Fletcher went on lecture tours to promote his theory that even liquids should be chewed many times.

## NO DIET FOR ME!

Not everyone wanted to follow a diet craze. Sylvester Graham, an American Presbyterian minister, inspired the Graham cracker to promote healthy living. He believed gluttony was destroying his country, so he advised a vegetable-based diet accompanied by bread or crackers, like the Graham cracker, made from coarse flour. He said people should drink only water.

The Graham cracker was inspired by the teachings of Sylvester Graham.

One person who did not take Graham's advice was Britain's Prince Regent, the future King George IV. He was so fat he was nicknamed the "Prince of Whales"!

Late in the nineteenth century, an American called James Buchanan Brady was as famous for his appetite as for the fortune he made on the railways. His breakfast was "eggs, breads, muffins, grits [boiled cornmeal], pancakes, steaks, chops, fried potatoes and pitchers of orange juice." Then he simply continued eating all day long!

Painters depicted George, the Prince Regent, as being slimmer than he actually was.

[25]

# THAT'S
## - ROMANTIC -

During the nineteenth century men and women who followed the Romantic art movement tried to look thin, pale and interesting.

One of the heroes of the Romantic movement was the English poet Lord Byron. Byron was naturally slightly chubby – but he was also extremely vain. He believed that being thin would keep his mind sharp, but he struggled to keep his weight down.

## THE MAD POET

Byron tried all sorts of ways to lose weight. He wore lots of clothes to make himself sweat, but being naturally greedy, he had to stop himself from bingeing on food. One of his favourite slimming meals was biscuits and soda water. He refused to dine with friends, preferring to stick to a fad diet of potatoes covered in vinegar. The dieting paid off. In five years Byron lost more than 22 kilograms (50 pounds)!

Lord Byron took up fencing as a form of exercise to help reduce his weight.

## PALE – BUT NOT INTERESTING

Byron was accused of setting a bad example for the young. His fans drank vinegar to lose weight and ate rice to make their complexions as pale as possible. Some girls hoped to fall ill so that they would lose weight. However, most people now understood that they could lose weight by eating less and exercising more. A French gourmet and politician called Jean Anthelme Brillat-Savarin, for example, championed a low-**carbohydrate** diet. Obsessed with losing stomach fat, he restricted his food intake. Brillat-Savarin believed that carbohydrates were the main cause of fat.

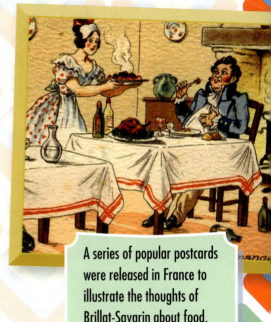

A series of popular postcards were released in France to illustrate the thoughts of Brillat-Savarin about food.

## hello Beautiful

During her youth in the first half of the nineteenth century, Queen Victoria (right) was fashionably thin, like fans of Lord Byron. Her tiny waist measured just 59 centimetres (22 inches). In 1861, however, Victoria's beloved husband Prince Albert died. She began to eat as a form of **consolation**. Over the years, her waist grew to a whopping 1.27 metres (50 inches)!

# COUNTING
## - CALORIES -

Once the connection was made between food intake and weight, it was only a matter of time before someone worked out which foods made people fat.

William Banting, funeral director to the royal family in the middle of the nineteenth century, was as fat as a barrel. He tried all sorts of diets and other measures to get rid of what he called "the evil" – his fat. From taking 90 steaming hot Turkish baths in a month to hours of intense exercise. But nothing worked.

Fatty fish and chips became a popular, cheap meal in Britain in the late 1800s.

## "DOING A BANTING"

The turning point came when a physician gave Banting a new diet to try. Banting swapped his carbohydrate-rich diet for **protein**-based foods. He stopped eating bread, butter, milk, sugar, beer and potatoes. Instead, he just ate meat and vegetables. The new diet was so successful that Banting lost nearly a quarter of his body weight – 22 kilograms (50 pounds) – in less than a year.

Banting was so pleased with the results that he decided the diet deserved to be better known so that more people could benefit. He laid out the principles of the diet in a book entitled *Letter on* **Corpulence**, which was published in 1864. The diet was an instant hit in Britain and America. Soon everyone was "doing a Banting".

# to die for

Wilbur Olin Atwater discovered that the best way to measure a person's calorie use was to put them inside a large sealed room. (Atwater actually gave the room the more scientific name of "respiration calorimeter".) The hugely expensive machine measured the heat given off by people eating different diets and carrying out different activities inside.

## COUNTING THE CALORIES

A scientific approach to losing weight started when US agricultural chemist Wilbur Olin Atwater studied the work of German chemists who were working out the energy content of different foods, measured in calories. Atwater wrote a pamphlet for the US Department of Agriculture. It looked at food in a new way in terms of the energy it produced. People began to think about how many calories food contained and how much energy they used in their lives. Atwater's recommendations (2,300 calories a day for women and 2,830 calories a day for men) are similar to the figures used today (2,000 calories for women and 2,500 for men).

Guests prepare to leave a fashionable dinner party at the end of the nineteenth century.

# Chapter 5
# THE TWENTIETH
## - CENTURY -

*From the tapeworm diet to the cabbage diet and no-carb diet, the twentieth century was full of promises of weight loss. By the end of the century, people were no thinner.*

The twentieth century was a turning point in the scientific understanding of nutrition and dieting. It was also a century when many people, particularly children, suffered from **malnutrition** and obesity.

## HOW WE ATE

At the start of the century, families spent around 44 per cent of their income on food. By the end of the century, the figure was 10 per cent. At the start of the century, most meals used fresh ingredients. By its end, many people ate convenience meals and fast food.

The demands of feeding millions of soldiers forced scientists to come up with cheap but nutritious food.

# WORLD WARS

Food shortages during the World Wars forced scientists to come up with healthier diets. Food had to be sent to feed the soldiers fighting in World War I (1914–1918), which meant that there was less food for people at home in Britain. In 1918, the government introduced rationing, which was a fair way of sharing food out among the population. Sugar, meat, flour, butter, margarine and milk were all rationed. A daily ration of bread for a man, for example, was 450 g (1 pound). A weekly ration of butter or margarine was 100 g (4 ounces) per person. Rationing was also needed during World War II, and the government encouraged people to grow their own vegetables. This became known as "Dig for Victory" and people used every available space in gardens and parks to plant seeds.

## THE GREAT DEPRESSION

The biggest food crisis in the United States came with the Great Depression of the 1930s. Mass unemployment and the failure of wheat harvests left millions of Americans hungry and malnourished. Families grew what food they could, while charities opened soup kitchens to feed the hungry.

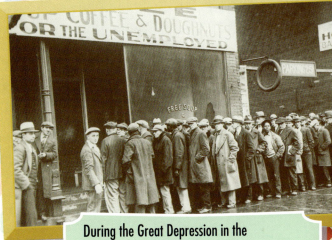

During the Great Depression in the United States, people who could not afford to buy food went to soup kitchens.

This World War II poster encourages people at home to recycle waste food for pigs.

# THAT'S
## - CONVENIENT -

*In the middle of the century,*
*a new food fashion burst onto the scene.*
*The television dinner had arrived and*
*eating would never be the same.*

This advertisement for TV dinners claims that its meals come from China, Italy, Mexico and Germany.

The road to the first TV dinner in 1954 was a long one. It began in 1810, when a British merchant patented the first tin can. Three years later the first commercial canning factory opened.

## ITS IN THE CAN

Canned foods were the first convenience foods. By the end of the nineteenth century, they were widely available. Frozen foods appeared in 1920, when Charles Birdseye started to deep freeze vegetables, fruit, fish and meats. Soon instant coffee, margarine (made from hydrogenated oil and chemical colouring) and instant mashed potato (powder that turned into grainy mash when boiling water was added) were all available. The selling point of such foods was convenience rather than nutrition. In the modern age, advertisers suggested, women needed fast food for their families.

## HEAT AND EAT

The convenience food revolution continued. **Microwave** technology led to a huge market in ready meals that could be heated in minutes and served. Individual TV dinners were served with parts of the meal in different sections of a plastic tray for heating and serving. Cooking fell out of fashion. Meals were no longer leisurely occasions. Now it was heat, eat and get on with watching TV or other leisure activities. Families no longer shopped locally; they went to large supermarkets and bought food with a long shelf life. Everything was meant to make life easier. Although food portions were small, people started to get fatter. In order to last longer and add flavour, convenience food was loaded with unseen sugars, salt and fat.

The microwave became popular after the first worktop model appeared in 1967.

# to die for

Expanding waistlines in the 1950s and 1960s called for drastic action. The narrow-waisted **hourglass** figure was back in fashion for women. Women reached for an accessory that had not been used for decades: the **corset**. Known as "waist slimmers", modern corsets promised to take 10 centimetres (4 inches) off a woman's waist. Breathe in!

THE "VERY THING" FOR LADIES
FOR AN ELEGANT FIGURE & GOOD HEALTH
HARNESS' MAGNETIC CORSETS
PRICE ONLY 5/6
POST FREE

FOR WOMEN OF ALL AGES

HARNESS' MAGNETIC CORSETS

5/6
LONDON. W.

The desire for a small waist sent women back to the corset that had been popular in the nineteenth century.

# FOOD IN
## - WARTIME -

*Many people ate better during the wars than at other times during the twentieth century. Food shortages and an emphasis on vegetables created a healthy diet.*

Many men who originally volunteered to fight in World War I were rejected because they were undernourished. Scientists soon worked out healthy and balanced diets to keep men on the front line as healthy as possible. Most of the time, however, the diet was boring and the portions small.

## A SOLDIER'S LOT

Soldiers on the Western Front ate tinned meat, which was usually "bully beef" – corned beef – with bread and biscuits. When real bread ran out, soldiers made their own fake bread from dried ground turnips. During World War II, US soldiers ate a lot better than their colleagues from Europe, where there were severe food shortages. US service personnel had chocolate bars in their rations. That made soldiers based in Europe a big hit with local people who had not tasted chocolate for years.

US soldiers have their teeth checked as part of a medical examination in World War I.

## THAT'S ALL!

In both world wars food supplies were rationed in both Britain and the United States to preserve vital supplies for soldiers. People were issued books of coupons they used to claim their weekly allowances. During World War II, Germany tried to starve Britain into surrender by reducing its imports of food across the Atlantic. Rationing was introduced in 1940 and lasted for 14 years, 9 years after the war itself had ended. Every man, woman and child was given a ration book containing coupons for rationed foods such as sugar, meat and cheese. Without coupons you could not buy these foods. Shoppers also had to register with certain shops.

A shopkeeper removes coupons from a ration book in return for food.

## to die for

In World War II, coffee was scarce. In Germany, people made ersatzkaffee, or "fake coffee", from barley, oats and chicory mixed with coal-oil tar. The British went without coffee. Americans fared better, although families were rationed to 450 grams (1 pound) of coffee every five weeks – less than a cup a day. People reused coffee grains to produce a watery drink nicknamed "Roosevelt coffee" after President Roosevelt.

# FAD
## - DIETS -

The twentieth century saw a whole series of diet crazes that were here today and gone tomorrow. They all promised weight loss and they all failed to deliver.

The century kicked off with the tapeworm diet and ended with the high-fat, low-carb diet. All the diets promised the same thing: weight loss without the effort of simply eating a healthy, balanced diet!

## A DIET A DAY

Eating tapeworms was the basis of the tapeworm diet! These parasites live inside the gut, so the theory is that they eat and digest food in your intestines, so you lose weight. If that didn't appeal, how about the Inuit diet of 1928? It recommended whale **blubber** – all you could eat. Even that was healthier than the Lucky Strike diet of 1925, which encouraged people to reach for a cigarette rather than a piece of chocolate. Other diets came sponsored by business, such as the banana-and-skimmed-milk diet produced by the United Fruit Company.

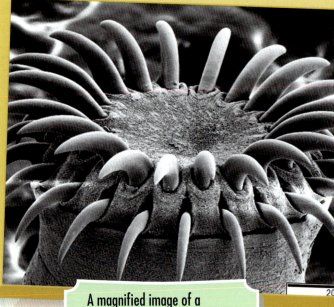

200

A magnified image of a tapeworm – would you let one live inside your stomach?

## DID IT WORK?

A series of different foods were promoted as the latest weight-loss miracle. On one diet of the 1930s, Hollywood stars ate grapefruit with every meal. The cabbage soup diet of the 1950s allowed unlimited amounts of food – as long as it was cabbage soup! The Atkins Diet and other diets followed the Banting diet and allowed their followers to eat unlimited amounts of protein – such as steak – and little else. People made millions from creating diets. In 1963, Jean Nidetch, an overweight housewife from New York, USA, devised a healthy weight-loss plan and launched Weight Watchers. Millions of people worldwide still attend Weight Watchers meetings today.

The grapefruit diet filled people up with water, which makes up 88 per cent of the fruit.

## hello beautiful

Different celebrities tried a number of diets. Rock and roll singer Elvis Presley struggled with obesity. He was said to have followed the sleep diet, which was popular in the 1970s. Patients were sedated so they would sleep for several days, during which they did not eat or drink. It was a drastic way of trying to lose weight!

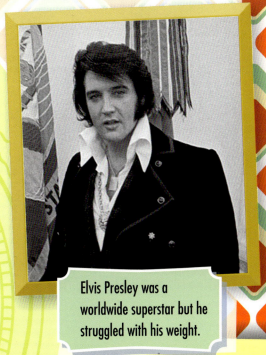

Elvis Presley was a worldwide superstar but he struggled with his weight.

# Chapter 6

# THE TWENTY-FIRST
## - CENTURY -

*Diets and dieting are just as confusing today as they were in the past. Diets come and go, but most people aren't getting any slimmer!*

Men and women have been thinking about their weight since the start of time. And they still are. Experts agree that modern life is making people fatter than ever.

## WHAT'S CHANGED?

With so much emphasis on making life easy, people have become lazy. Keeping slim has become hard work. Many families drive everywhere rather than walking. People sit all day in the office or at school and exercise for short periods, if at all. Fast food is available 24/7, but much of it is loaded with fat and sugar. At the same time, we are bombarded with images of idealized bodies. It's enough to make anyone reach for a comforting cookie!

The US fast-food chain McDonald's has restaurants in 119 countries, including here in St. Petersburg in Russia.

## I'M CONFUSED!

It is hardly surprising that most people are confused about which foods to eat. The last decades of the twentieth century were dominated by the idea that all fat was bad, and sugar was a good replacement for fat. We now know that some fats – healthy fats found in olive oil and avocados – are vital and sugar is bad. Most processed food has added sugar to make it taste better.

The question today remains what is "healthy eating" and how do we achieve it? The answer is actually simple: everything in moderation, as the Greeks worked out thousands of years ago. Eat lots of vegetables, a little protein and the odd sweet treat. Combine that with regular exercise and it becomes even easier to maintain a healthy weight.

# THE PERFECT
## - MODEL? -

*Today, the global fashion industry is worth billions of pounds. The faces of fashion are the super-thin models who strut the catwalk.*

**Experts estimate that if the fashion industry was ranked alongside countries' economies it would be the seventh largest economy in the world today.**

## A GLOBAL BUSINESS

To sell clothes, fashion houses put on catwalk shows and use models to display their latest creations. The fashion industry has always used very slim women as models because designers believe their clothes sit better on thinner women. However, a trend to use so-called size 0 models – models who were extremely thin – meant young models had to use extreme dieting. Girls trying to copy the look also ate unhealthily. The fashion world and young women more generally saw a general rise in **eating disorders**, such as anorexia nervosa and bulimia. Things began to change in the 2010s. Different fashion houses and fashion magazines finally acknowledged the problem of promoting unhealthy body ideals. They said they would no longer use underweight models.

Everyone is used to seeing slim models on the catwalk.

## SHE'S MY IDOL

Young women have always looked up to women in the public eye. Over the centuries, European royalty set the pace, then actresses and Hollywood stars. Today, many teenagers **idolize** young women who blog and vlog about fashion. Traditionally, advertisers have used young, slim women and men to sell products. With the internet's global reach and the popularity of reality TV, body images of stars are becoming varied. The biggest stars of the last few years, the Kardashians, have shown that the super-slim physique may finally be on its way out.

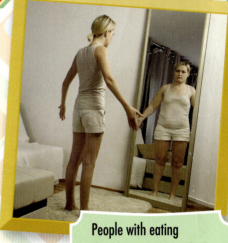

People with eating disorders see themselves as being larger than they actually are.

American model Ashley Graham has been on the cover of lots of glossy magazines, including *Cosmopolitan* and *British Vogue*. What makes her unusual is that she is a size 14 in an industry where size 6 is considered large! Graham thinks of herself as a body activist who is working hard to change people's perception of women's size.

Ashley Graham is one of a group of curvier models challenging normal fashion ideas of how women should look.

# BACK TO
## - THE PAST -

*Want to eat like a caveman by grabbing a piece of meat and some berries? If so, you would be joining one of the latest fashionable diets.*

**Eager to persuade people that they can lose weight easily, dietary experts and those hoping to make money encourage those who want to lose weight to look back to a time when, they imagine, everyone was much slimmer and healthier.**

## EAT WHAT?

A whole range of fashionable diets at the start of the twenty-first century looked back to simpler forms of life. They included the Palaeo (caveman) diet and a revival of the Inuit diet (high protein, with no fruit and vegetables). Claiming to be based on what people in the Bible would have eaten, the Hallelujah diet advises only eating raw plant-based foods. Another very popular diet is the 5:2 diet, which is based on **intermittent** fasting. People eat normally for five days of the week, but eat a minimal amount of food for the other two days.

Fish dry in the open air in an Inuit settlement. The animal-based Inuit diet became briefly popular around 2015.

## BLINDED BY SCIENCE

Most people who diet want to be healthy, and look and feel better. But dieting in the twenty-first century is very difficult. Processed foods are full of hidden fats and sugars. Manufacturers claim foods are healthy even when they are not. A stream of scientific arguments promotes one way of eating or another.

More than at any time in history, however, eating well should be easy. There is a wider variety of fresh food than ever before, as long as people know what to look for. Losing weight is as simple as it was in ancient Greece: take in fewer calories than you burn up. To do that, there is no need to spend money on diet books. You only need to be sensible – and that comes free!

Extreme dieting of any form is now generally recognized as unhealthy.

## to die for

Anorexia nervosa is a psychiatric illness that causes people to starve themselves to try to achieve what they see as a better body image. Most sufferers are girls and young women aged from 15 to 24. Anorexia can be treated, but when left untreated it has the highest death rate of any psychiatric illness.

Although anorexia is called an eating disorder, doctors say it is actually a mental illness.

# -TIMELINE-

**c.600 BC** The followers of the philosopher Pythagoras become vegetarians and give up eating beans.

**478 BC** Hatshepsut comes to the throne in Egypt. She suffers clogged arteries from her rich diet.

**c.400 BC** The Greek physician Hippocrates writes about the balance between eating food and doing exercise.

**c.00s AD** Marcus Gavius Apicius is a famous gourmet in Rome. One of his favourite delicacies is flamingo tongues.

**c.400 AD** A cookbook is created. It is a collection of Roman recipes that is often named after Apicius.

**c.500** Saint Benedict imposes strict dietary rules on monks to demonstrate their commitment to Christ.

**c.1100** The Crusades in the Middle East open new routes to bring spices to Europe from Asia.

**c.1475** Italian author Il Platina writes the first printed cookbook.

**1520s** Europeans build the first sugar mills on the islands of the Caribbean, which becomes a major source of imported sugar in Europe.

**1558** The Venetian writer Luigi Cornaro writes *The Art of Living*, the first known diet book.

**1589** English explorer Sir Walter Raleigh plants potatoes in Ireland, having brought them from South America. Within a few decades potatoes become a staple food in Europe.

| | |
|---|---|
| c.1630 | Flemish artist Peter Paul Rubens paints women with full, fleshy figures. |
| 1771 | King Adolf Frederick of Sweden dies after eating a huge meal. |
| 1806 | The Romantic poet Lord Byron begins a diet and launches a fashion for living on soda water and potatoes in vinegar. |
| 1810 | A British manufacturer takes out a patent for tinned food. |
| 1825 | The French politician Jean Anthelme Brillat-Savarin promotes a low-carbohydrate diet. |
| 1864 | Funeral director William Banting starts a diet craze when he writes a book describing his own weight loss. |
| 1890s | Horace Fletcher promotes Fletcherizing, a diet based on chewing food. |
| 1896 | Wilbur Olin Atwater begins to analyse the calorific content of foods. |
| 1914 | At the outbreak of World War I, armies find that many recruits are too undernourished to serve in the military. |
| 1920 | Horace Birdseye begins to freeze food to store it. |
| 1939 | World War II begins in Europe. During the conflict, food rationing is widespread – it actually leads to people eating a more healthy diet. |
| 1954 | The first TV dinners are introduced in the United States. |
| 1963 | US housewife Jean Nidetch launches Weight Watchers, which remains highly popular throughout the world. |
| 2010s | Fashion designers and magazines respond to public pressure by reducing their use of "size 0" models, who are widely thought to set poor examples for body-conscious young women. |

# -GLOSSARY-

**amphitheatre** Roman stadium

**blubber** thick layer of fat in animals such as whales and seals

**calories** scientific units for measuring the energy content of food

**carbohydrate** compound in food such as sugar or starch that can be broken down into energy

**civilizations** societies with advanced organization and culture

**conquistadors** Spanish adventurers in the Americas in the sixteenth century

**consolation** something that helps people recover from a loss

**corpulence** state of being fat

**corset** undergarment fastened with laces, worn to shape the waist

**Crusades** wars between Christians and Muslims in the Holy Land in the twelfth and thirteenth centuries

**devout** very religious

**diabetes** condition in which the human body struggles to or cannot produce a hormone called insulin

**eating disorders** psychological problems that lead to disturbed eating habits

**fad** widespread but brief enthusiasm for something

**gluttony** greed or excess in eating

**hourglass** shape with a rounded top and bottom and a narrow middle

**idolize** admire or respect someone

**immortal** living forever

**indulgent** quick to give in to your own desires and appetites

**infectious** describing a disease that spreads easily among people

**intermittent** happening at irregular intervals

**lacquer** hard, transparent coating used for wood

**laxatives** drugs that make people go to the toilet

**malnutrition** lack of proper nutrition, usually caused by eating too little or too much

**microwave** oven that heats food by stimulating radio waves

**mummies** dead bodies that are dried and preserved

**noblewoman** woman from the privileged class at the top of society

**nutritional** related to the process of consuming food for growth

**obese** very fat or overweight

**parasites** organisms that live by taking food from other organisms

**protein** part of food found in meat, milk, eggs and beans

**rationed** limited the distribution of food to individuals in times of shortage

**saturated fats** unhealthy fats found in some foods

**stools** pieces of faeces

**suckling pigs** young pigs that are cooked whole

**vegetarians** people who do not eat meat

**vision quest** Native American ritual intended to inspire visions